Journey Through History

Modern Times

Translation: Jean Grasso Fitzpatrick

English translation © Copyright 1988 by Barron's Educational Series, Inc.

© Parramón Ediciones, S.A.
First Edition, February 1988
The title of the Spanish edition is *La edad moderna*

All inquiries should be addressed to:
Barron's Educational Series, Inc.
250 Wireless Boulevard
Hauppauge, New York 11788

Library of Congress Catalog Card No. 88-10388
International Standard Book No. 0-8120-3392-2
Library of Congress Cataloging-in-Publication Data

Vergés, Gloria.
  [Edad moderna. English]
  Modern times / [illustrated by] María Rius ; [written by] Gloria &
Oriol Vergés ; [translation, Jean Grasso Fitzpatrick]. — 1st ed.
    p. cm. — (Journey through history)
  Translation of: Edad moderna.
  Summary: An introductory history of the seventeenth and eighteenth
centuries, with a fictional story involving children to depict the
era.
  ISBN 0-8120-3392-2
  1. History, Modern—17th century–Juvenile literature.
2. History, Modern-18th century–Juvenile literature.
[1. History, Modern–17th century.   2. History, Modern–18th
century.]   I. Rius, María, ill.   II. Vergés, Oriol.   III. Title.
IV. Series: Vergés, Gloria. Viaje a través de la historia.
English.
D247.V4713 1988
909.6–dc19   88-10388
                                                       CIP
                                                        AC

Printed in Spain by Sirven Grafic
Legal Deposit: B-39.934-88

90   98765432

Journey Through History

Modern Times

María Rius
Glòria & Oriol Vergés

BARRON'S

New York • Toronto • Sydney

The power of European rulers grew, and, with the help of their ministers, they controlled the wealth of their countries. They believed that they had been chosen as kings by God, and, therefore, they need answer to no one. To avoid plots against them, they had the nobles live in the royal palaces. They gave them important political responsibilities and invited them to the great court festivals celebrated in lavish halls decorated by great artists.

"This palace of Versailles is the most splendid in the world."
"Maybe, but I prefer the gardens—with their flowers, fountains, and sculptures."

The world of music was changing rapidly. In addition to the religious works that were sung in churches, musicians composed pieces to be played in the homes of the nobility and the wealthy. New instruments appeared, such as the violin, the cello, and the piano. And musicians became well-known and admired.

In Holland, England, and France, companies were organized to trade with India and the East. They raised money to pay for each voyage. When the ship returned home, the investors shared in the profits. In this way, people who were not members of the nobility grew very wealthy. Some of them rose to positions of political power in the cities.

"When this expedition returns in a few months, I will be even richer. Maybe then I will become mayor of the city, and perhaps I will end up being governor of the province."

"Then I hope you'll make sure our city becomes the most beautiful in the country."

"My father says that Parliament in London is just as important as the king."

"That's true. The king can't pass any law if it hasn't been approved first by Parliament."

In England all groups of the population—nobles, merchants, and craftsmen—were represented in Parliament. This political system was different from that of other European countries, and it allowed the king to be in constant touch with his subjects.

The English people today are very proud of their traditions and their past.

In France, a group of brilliant philosophers stated that all people were free and had rights that no one could take away. Furthermore, they said that the opinion of the citizens and peasants was worth more than that of the kings and nobles.

They also believed that individual liberty should be respected, and that all people should live together without any one group ruling over the rest.

These were the principles of democracy, an important force in most of the world today.

In North America, the colonies, although dependent on England, developed their own ways of life. In the end, they declared and fought for their independence. After the war they founded the United States of America, the first nation under a democratic system.

In the United States, everyone had his or her own responsibility. By working together, they made the new North American states grow into one great country.

"Grandmother, is it true that George Washington was a very important man?"

"Yes. He led the colonists in the Revolutionary War against England and was the first President of the United States."

In many parts of Europe, people met in the woods or fields to sing, dance, or play, and forget the worries of daily life. They showed off their best clothes. Some nobles also joined in the party.

Francisco de Goya, a great Spanish painter, captured all the color and grace of these popular events in a series of paintings filled with life and movement.

"I like these afternoons at the feast very much. Everyone is happy and in high spirits."

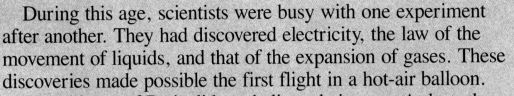

During this age, scientists were busy with one experiment after another. They had discovered electricity, the law of the movement of liquids, and that of the expansion of gases. These discoveries made possible the first flight in a hot-air balloon.

The citizens of Paris did not believe their eyes. At last, the ancient dream that people could fly like birds had come true—a dream people had had from the time of the Greeks through the Middle Ages and the Renaissance.

"I wouldn't go up off the ground for anything!"

"Well, I would. The people who built the balloon, the Montgolfier brothers, say that, according to the laws of physics, there's no way it will fall."

When the citizens of Paris learned the new philosophical theories, they proclaimed their right to liberty and political equality. It was then that the French Revolution took place, which was the start of a new age in the history of Europe. One of the first acts of the revolution was the storming of the Bastille, a prison that represented the absolute power of the kings and nobility.

The revolution was very violent, but the political principles on which it was founded are the foundation of today's democracy.

"Our revolution will change many things according to the principle: "Liberty, equality, fraternity."

"You're right. The reign of the nobility has ended!"

The railroad, with its great speed, was an important advance in the transportation of goods and passengers. Now the newly-built factories could more easily deliver their products to cities and to ports from which they could be shipped abroad. At the same time, people who lived in remote towns and cities could visit their relatives and friends more often.

Little by little the railroad contributed to the growth of towns along its route, where new factories and more businesses were built.

Railways extended rapidly through many countries, despite the fact that many peasants were afraid of the locomotives.

"The smoke and the sparks that these machines throw off will burn our harvests."

"They look like the work of the devil!"

Most of the textile factories that were built in Europe used cotton that had been grown in fields in the United States. Harvesting cotton was tricky. It had to be done quickly, since storms could damage the crop, and for that reason many workers were needed.

At first, the fields were worked by black slaves who were badly treated by the plantation owners. To console themselves about their miserable situation, they sang very emotional songs with religious themes. Today we call them "spirituals."

"How hard our life is!"

"That's true, but my daddy says that the day will come when black people will be free! I believe him. Some day we'll have the same rights as the whites do!"

Factories changed the landscape of many parts of Europe and North America. The tall smokestacks by the rivers and in the cities represented a new system where people worked together in large buildings.

Many children worked in the factories with grown men and women. Life for these workers was very hard. They earned very low wages and were not paid when they were sick, injured, or too old to work.

"Every day more peasants come to work in the new factories."

"That makes sense. Even though the workers put in long hours for little pay, at least they don't have to worry about bad harvests."

"It doesn't seem possible that we could hear music through this gadget!"

The industrial era changed the way of life of people who lived in Europe and North America. There was a race to advance science and invent new machines that is still going on today. Like the phonograph, each invention seemed completely extraordinary until it was surpassed by something even better.

Little by little, our great-grandparents became used to the new inventions and enjoyed them.

Today they no longer amaze us, and we would probably not know how to live without the conveniences they offer.

Absolute monarchies

Children should focus on the modern age as one in which a series of changes took place that affected the ways of life of their grandparents, their parents, and even themselves. Louis XIV of France, the Sun King, was the outstanding example of an absolute monarch. Absolute monarchs believed that the king's power was derived directly from God.

Baroque Art and Music

The baroque period (the seventeenth and eighteenth centuries) was typified by movement in the curved and broken forms of buildings, sculptures, and paintings. It was also an age in which music took new directions, in instrumental and choral compositions. Two names stand out—Johann Sebastian Bach and Wolfgang Amadeus Mozart. Mozart.

The Rise of the European Bourgeoisie

Commerce had considerably enriched the middle class, which now wanted greater political representation. Up until now it had participated in city governments, but power was held by the nobility. In England, the parliamentary system set an example for the rest of Europe.

The New Theories of French Philosophers

French philosophers of the eighteenth century were already advancing political and social theories that prevail today in most modern states: democracy and the separation of the three branches of government, legislative, executive, and judicial. These ideas were not looked upon favorably by the nobility or the clergy, nor of course by the absolute monarchy.

The Birth of North America

On the other side of the Atlantic, English colonists organized themselves socially and politically in accord with the new French philosophical theories. The American Constitution and the Bill of Rights opened paths to freedom that European politicians later followed.

Daily Life in the Eighteenth Century

Ordinary people enjoyed popular festivals in which the nobility and upper classes also participated. Scientists did experiments in their laboratories on the laws of physics concerning gases, liquids, and electricity. All of their scientific advances amazed the citizens, who scarcely believed what they were seeing.

The Great Political Change in France

The French Revolution was the political event that marked the beginning of a new age. The people of Paris and other French cities, led by the educated bourgeoisie, started a revolution that became the seed of social and political upheavals ever since. Napoleon Bonaparte, military and political leader, inherited revolutionary France but failed in his intention to dominate Europe.

The Applications of the Steam Engine

Steam energy led to the Industrial Revolution and revolutionized transport systems with the development of railroads and steamboats. From then on, railway systems were tied to industrial expansion, to the improvement of commerce, and to communication between people. Steam was the energy source that set the Industrial Revolution in motion.

The Industrial Era

Coal (for steam engines) and steel (for construction) were indispensable elements in the Industrial Revolution. Cotton from the United States, India, or Egypt was the raw material that permitted the establishment of factories, first in England and then in the rest of Europe. With industrialization, two new social classes appeared: the industrial bourgeoisie and the working class.